> The millennium celebrations required an iconic structure.

> The Dome is a response to a site, a climate, a timescale.

>Shelter
>The Dome is
>a shelter:
an enclosed open
space. It moderates
extremes of
climate.

> The Dome acts like an umbrella.
It protects visitors against wind, rain and sun.
The Dome roof also allowed construction of exhibits
to proceed unhindered by outside conditions.

> Shelter

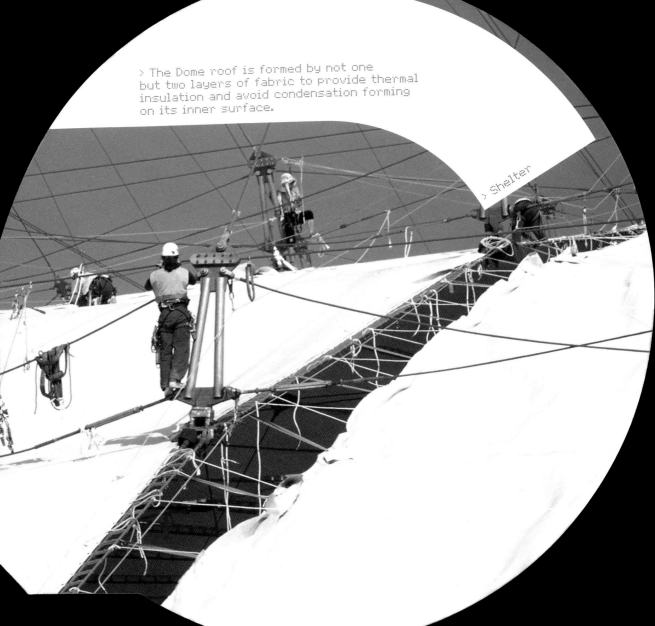

> The Dome roof is formed by not one but two layers of fabric to provide thermal insulation and avoid condensation forming on its inner surface.

> Shelter

> Designing a building to go within a weather-proof enclosure poses a question. What does that building have to be? Does it need a roof, windows, walls, doors?

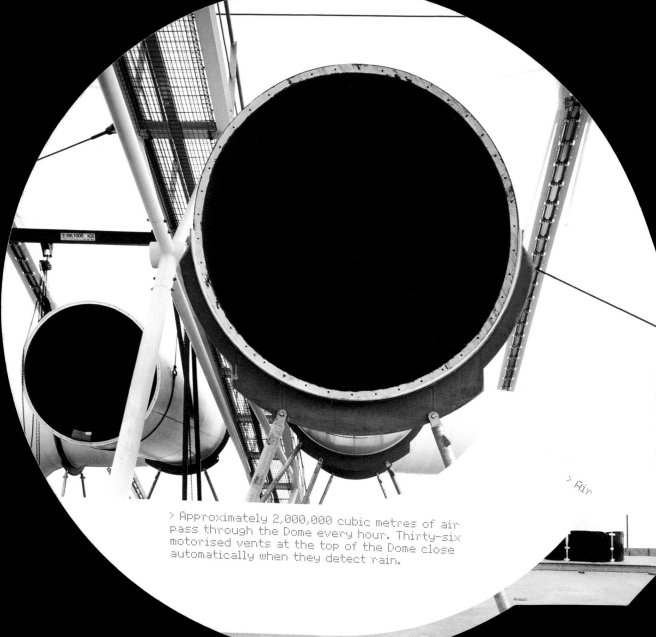

> Air

> Approximately 2,000,000 cubic metres of air pass through the Dome every hour. Thirty-six motorised vents at the top of the Dome close automatically when they detect rain.

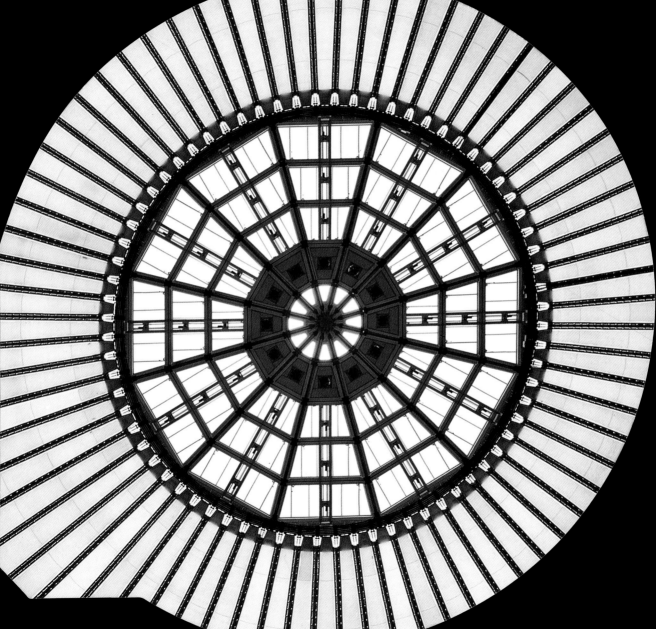

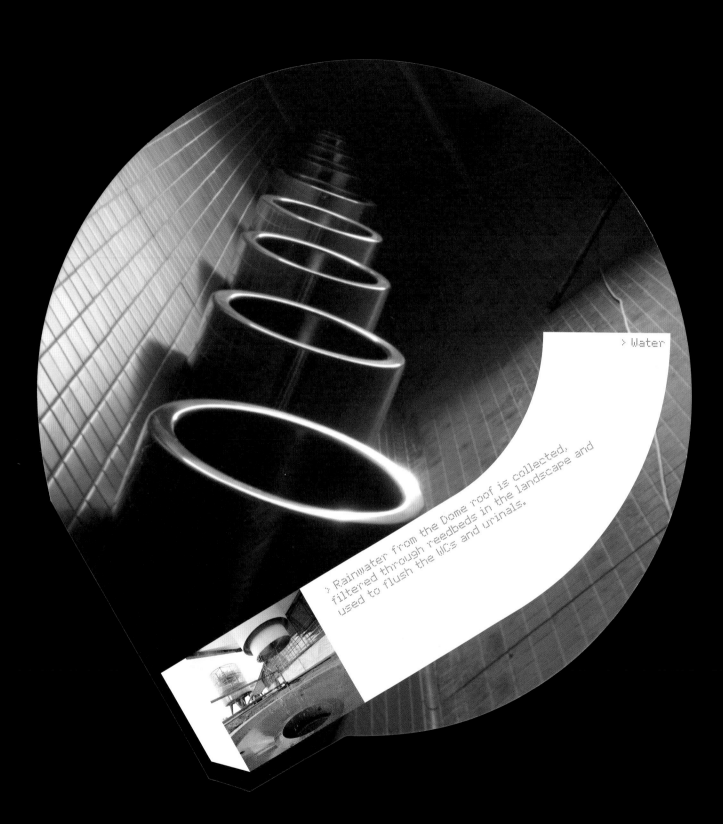

> Water

> Rainwater from the Dome roof is collected, and filtered through reedbeds in the landscape, and used to flush the WCs and urinals.

> The landscape around the Dome is predominately planted with native species that can survive the harsh conditions of the Greenwich peninsula

> Landscape

> Definition

> Reedbeds help to filter water from the Dome roof. Every day 500,000 litres of water can be reclaimed.

> Scala

> The Dome is a response to a 300-acre
site bounded by the sweep of the river Thames.
Its full extent is only visible from above.

> The service pods and the scalloped edge of the fabric are designed to help give visitors a sense of scale at ground level.

> Scale

> The curve of the Dome roof makes its size difficult to read. The closer you get, the less you can see, and so the smaller the Dome appears to be.

Door II

Roof:
50 metres high
Diameter:
365 metres
Circumference:
1km

> Scale is difficult to assimilate inside the Dome. It contains no familiar features and so there is nothing with which to compare it.

> Balance

> Forces of tension and compression are in
absolute balance in the Dome. The structure is
a cable net. Each cable is in tension.

> Balance

> The cables are pulled into the air by the masts and held down by anchor blocks attached to a ring beam.

Balance
Each mast is in
compression

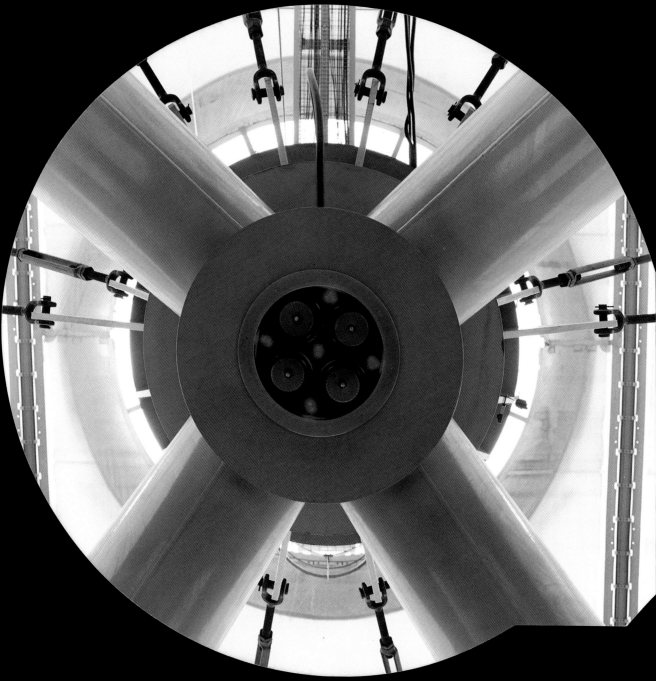

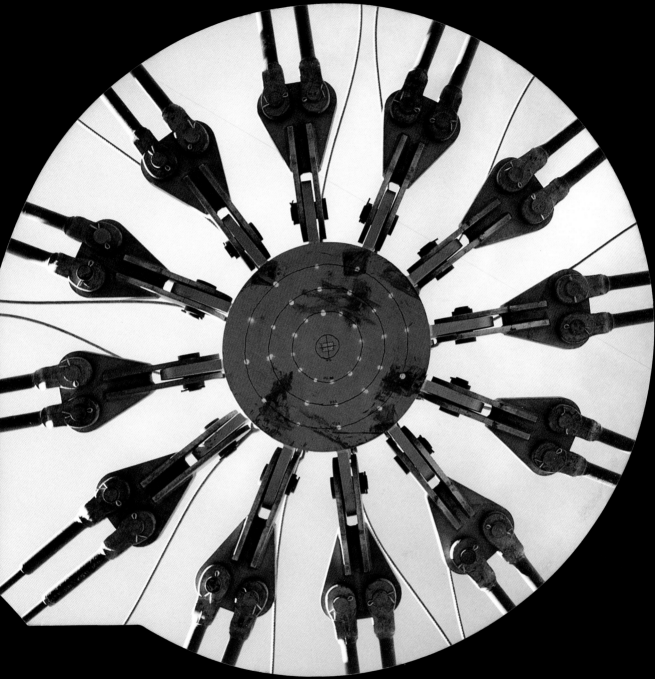

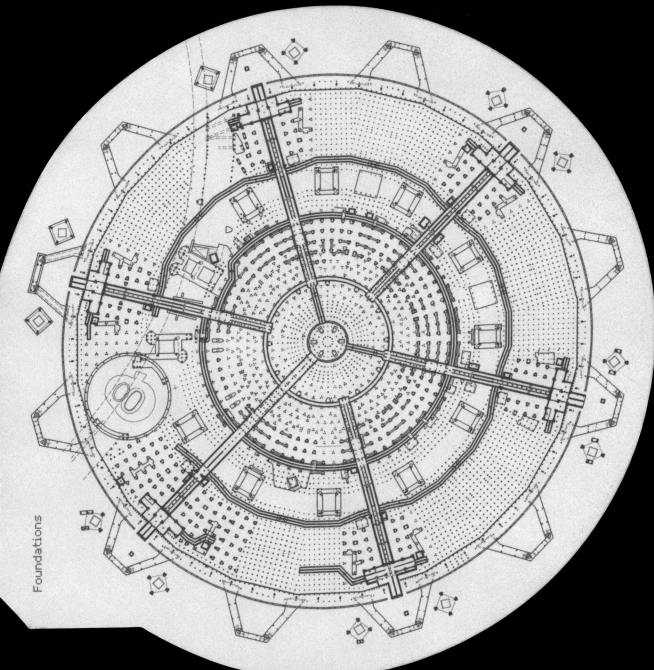

Foundations

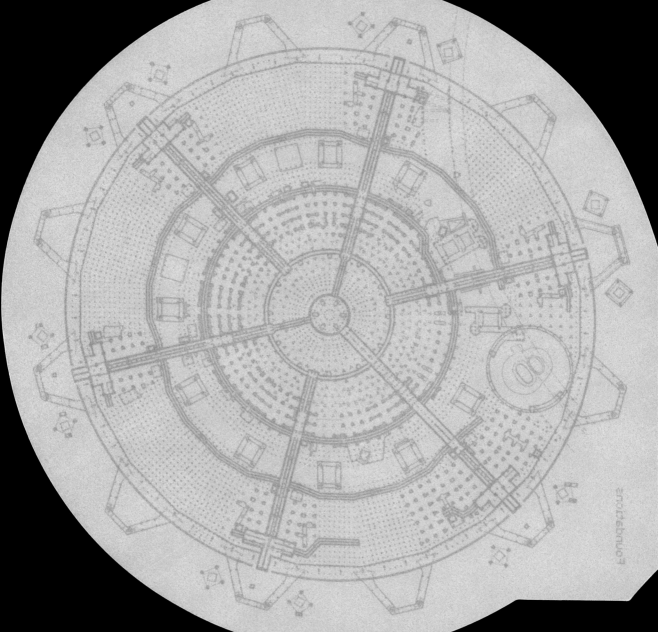

Foundations

Masts

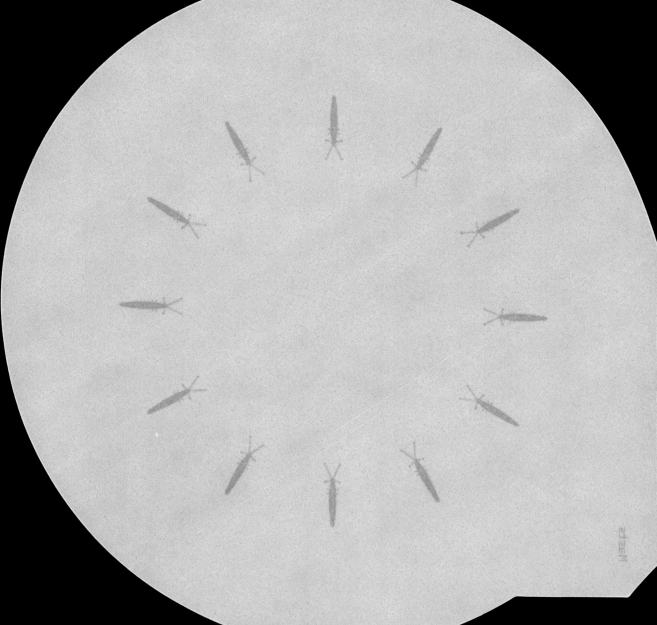

Cable Net

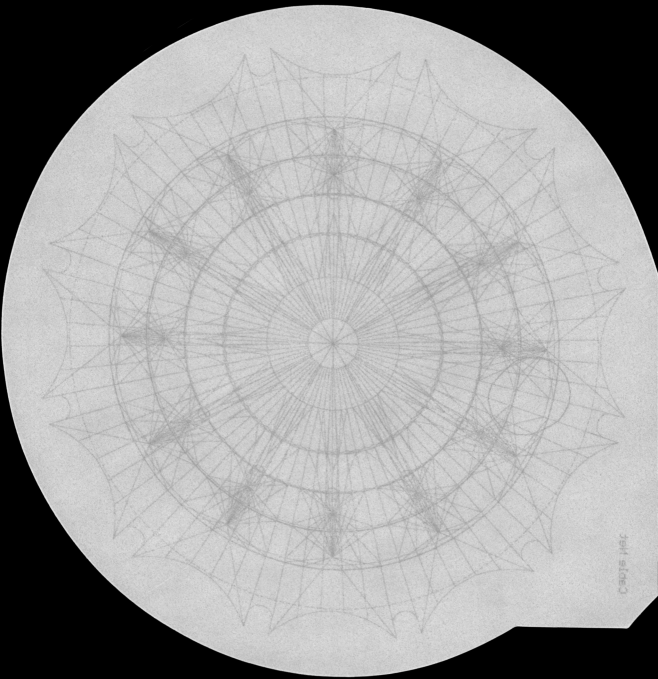

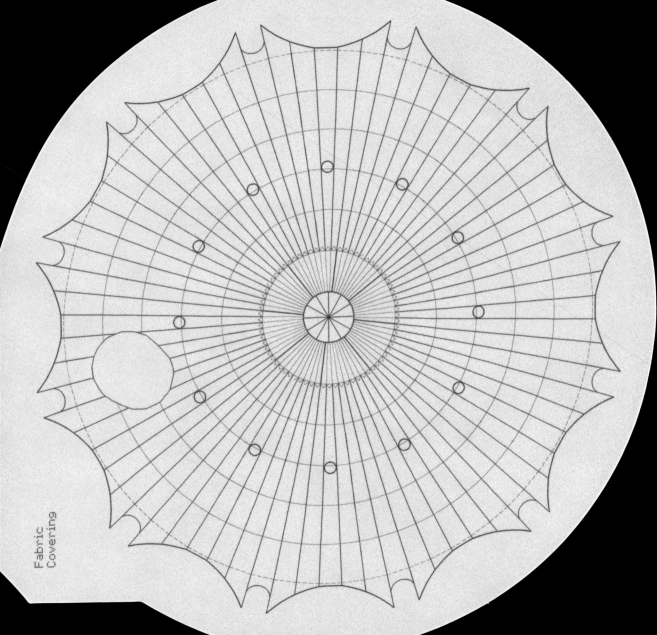

Fabric
Covering

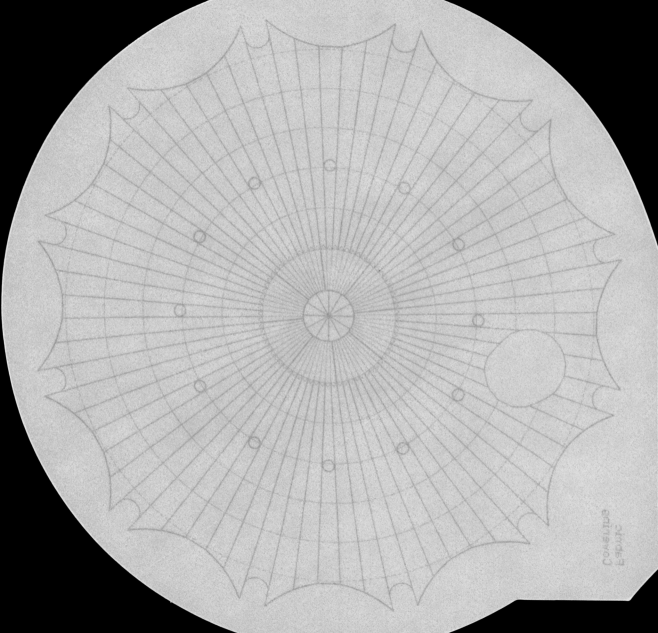

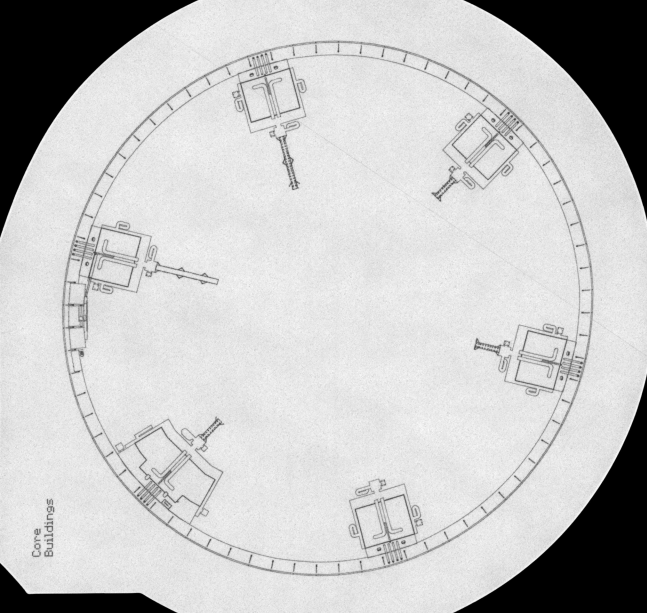

Core
Buildings

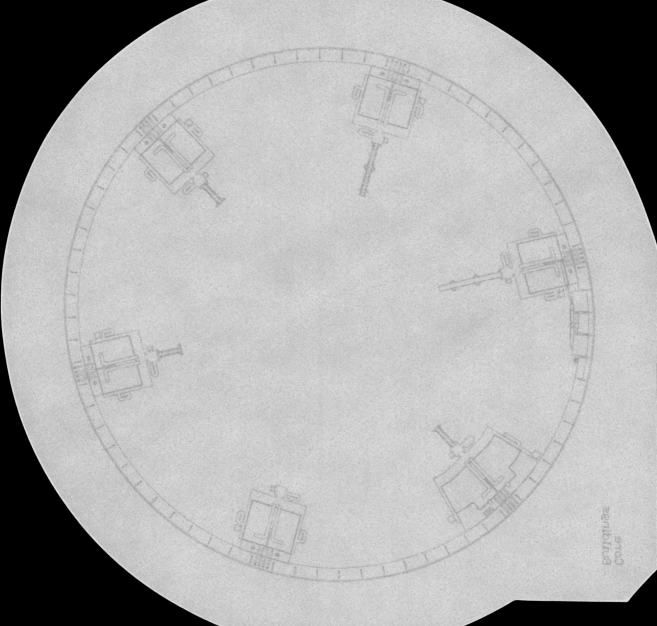

Central
Promenade

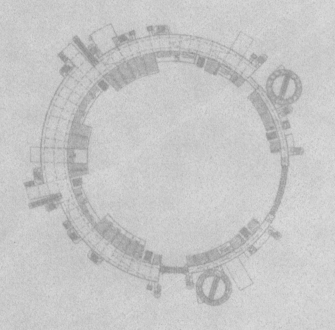

Internal
Road

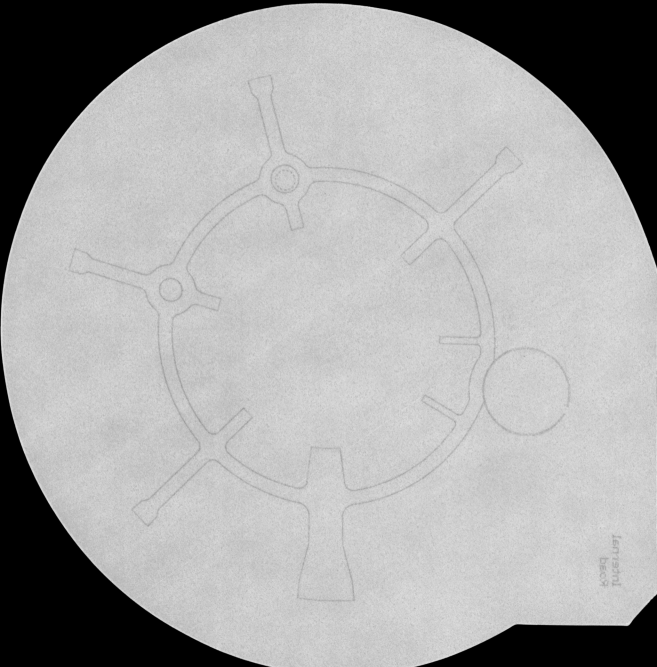

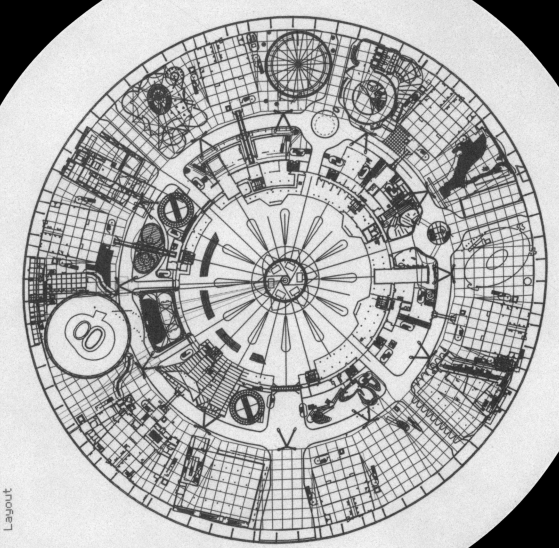

Exhibition
Layout

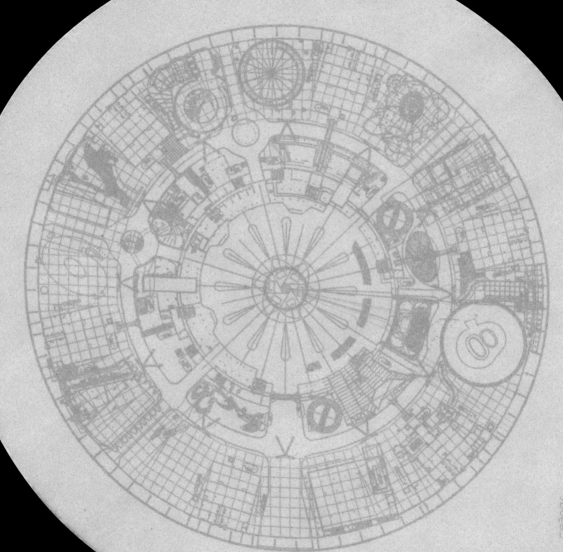

Exhibition
Layout

> Balance

>The tension in the Dome roof is equivalent to the pull of twenty jumbo jets at full thrust.

> As the Dome's structure is in perfect balance, very little material is needed to make it stable — the total weight of the masts, cables and fabric cladding is less than a 12m cube of water.

> Materials

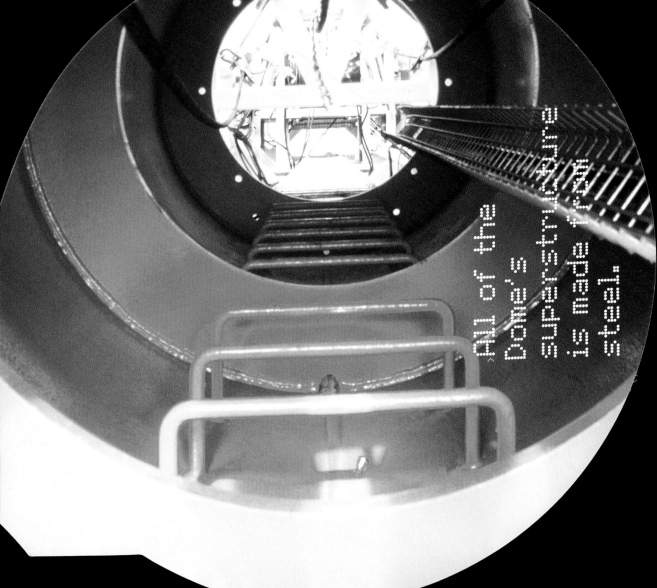

All of the Dome's superstructure is made from steel.

Materials
The cladding is
1mm thick teflon-
coated glass fibre.

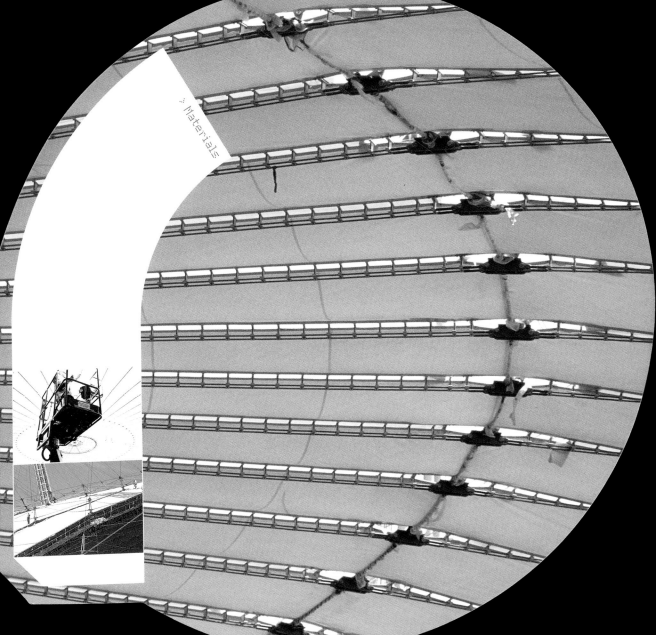

Materials

> The Atomic Energy Authority's computers were used to predict the flow of air and heat around the Dome.

> Technology

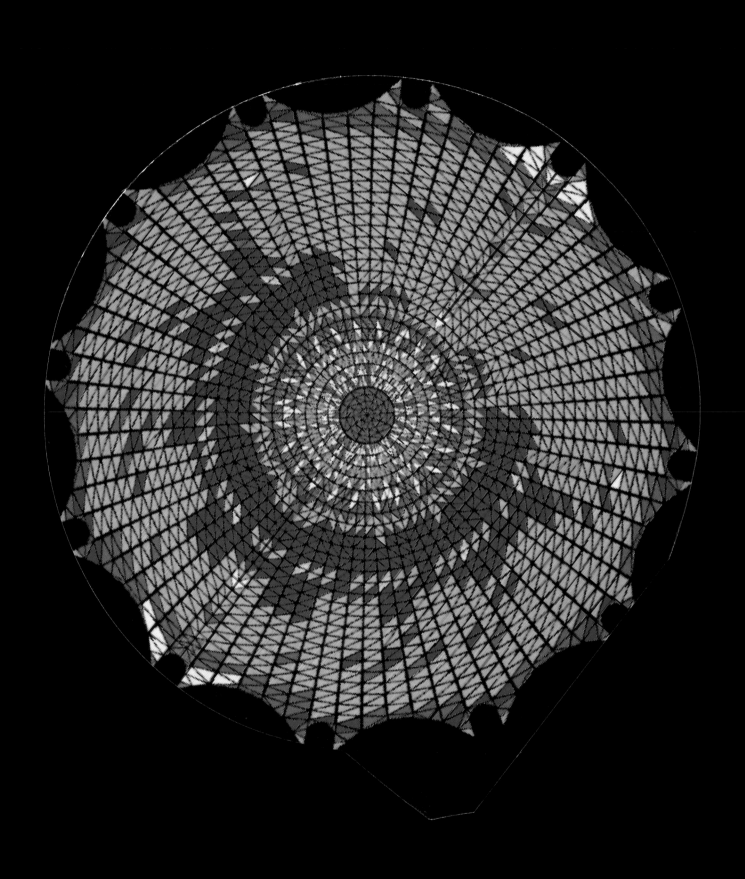

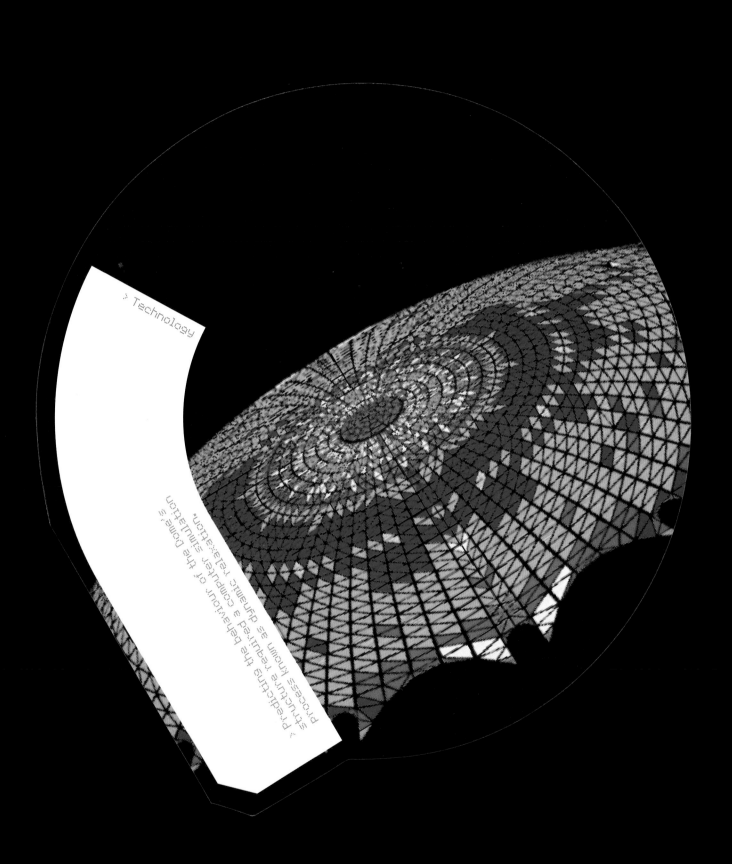

> Predicting the behaviour as dynamic structure known as dynamic relaxation.
"Noticing the behaviour of the Dome's process required a computer simulation.

Definition

When construction began, no final decisions had been used about the Dome would actually be content or of the likely use of the site after the Millennium Experience

> More than 8,000 concrete piles were put in the ground to allow virtually anything to be built above.

> Design of the foundations, electrical infrastructure, service trenches and core buildings had to be finalised before their exact use was known.

> Definition

> To maximise the available area, the Dome extends over the Blackwall Tunnel ventilation shaft which protrudes through the roof.

> The vent is enclosed to prevent fumes escaping into the Dome

> The futures exchange was consulted to evaluate likely resale values of building services plant, and some items were selected on this basis.

> Definition

:People
:The Dome structure
was complete in just
one year

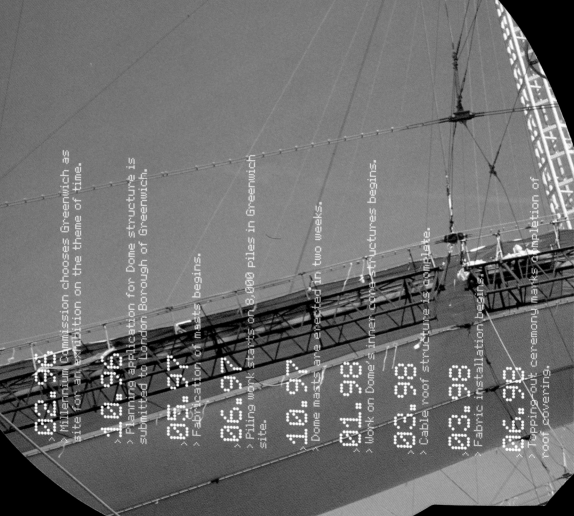

02:96
> Millennium Commission chooses Greenwich as site for an exhibition on the theme of time.

10:96
> Planning application for Dome structure is submitted to London Borough of Greenwich.

05:97
> Fabrication of masts begins.

06:97
> Piling work starts on 8,000 piles in Greenwich site.

10:97
> Dome masts are erected in two weeks.

01:98
> Work on Dome's inner core structures begins.

03:98
> Cable roof structure is complete.

03:98
> Fabric installation begins.

06:98
> Topping-out ceremony marks completion of roof covering.

> Acknowledgements

> Client: New Millennium Experience Company
> Architect: Richard Rogers Partnership
> Engineer: Buro Happold
> Construction: McAlpine Laing Joint Venture

> Book Design: North

First published in 2000 by Booth Clibborn
Editions Limited
12 Percy Street, London W1P 9FB
www.booth-clibborn-editions.co.uk

Printed and bound in Hong Kong
ISBN 1-86154-148-1

©NMEC 2000
NMEC Logo ©1998

Chronology

> Dome opens to public.

01.00

> Dome structure is complete.

02.99

> Construction of exhibition zones begins.

11.98